Success is 1% plan, 99% action.

GREETINGS, MY FRIEND AND READER, IT IS MY GREAT PLEASURE TO SHARE MY OBSERVATIONS WITH YOU.

Today will be
a good day

The information presented in this book covers a variety of topics, emphasizing the importance of positivity, joy, and family in the workplace, as well as the significance of goal-setting in various life domains. The texts highlight the role of salesmanship in business and provide insights into becoming an unstoppable salesperson. Other themes include efficient management over empire-building, avoiding excessive paperwork, the value of teaching within a company, overcoming idea destroyers for innovation, and essential tasks for personal and professional growth, such as self-investment and understanding life cycles. The main message of the book revolves around becoming a leader in business and within a team, encouraging readers to use the book as a guide for leadership development by applying its teachings in daily life.

creator: Sergii

WHY YOU SHOULD READ THIS BOOK

If you bought this book, it means you have a desire to move forward. If someone gave you a book, it means you want to improve. Having a desire to improve, to make your mark, to make changes, to grow professionally, to become more successful, to become a leader is good. A leader is a person who bears strategic responsibility for the well-being and future of the organization. The leader can be a director, chief, queen or governor. Regardless of the name, it means chief. If you want to become a leader, this book will help you.

The path to the top is influenced by countless factors: your work habits, luck, sense of timing, your competitors, your personality, the people who support you, your talent, circumstances, and so on. This book will help you improve your work habits, influence external circumstances, sharpen your sense of timing, stay ahead of your competitors, and maximize your talent. This is a book of tips and tricks. The ideas you will find in it are based on the real business world. They are fresh, direct, honest, without bias, easy to read, easy to understand and easy to implement.

Many recommendations take the form of rules and commandments, and this is because it should be so, not because it can be so. Although the content of the book is intended to help you advance in the company, you can use the observations and advice outside of work, in your free time.

The surest way to a leading position is to buy a company or open your own. If you are planning a career in a large company, this book will help you. Even if you want to start your own business, this book will help you a lot.

GOOD LEADER

In business, money is like a pendant you wear. The more you earn, the better you are. It's simple.

ALWAYS GO FOR THE HIGHEST SALARY JOB

After you have figured out what you want to do, whether it's banking, advertising, manufacturing, or something else, get a job at a company that offers you the highest salary.

If you haven't decided on a specific career or field yet, take the position where you'll earn the most. If you're working in a large company, always opt for transfers and promotions or a job that pays the best.

There are several important reasons to go after the money.

Firstly, all your bonuses and increments will be calculated based on your salary. Companies calculate all salary increases in percentages, so a ten percent increase on twenty-two thousand dollars is two hundred dollars more than the same salary increase on twenty thousand dollars.

Secondly, the higher you are paid, the more notice you get from the company's management.

Thirdly, the more money you earn, the more is expected of you. This means more responsibility, more tasks, and more problems to solve. The opportunity to prove yourself is an invitation to success.

Fourthly, if there are two candidates vying for a promotion to a position with a fifty-thousand-dollar salary, and the first one earns forty thousand dollars a year, and the second one earns thirty thousand, the higher-paid candidate will always win the position. Higher-paid individuals will get the job regardless of talent, diligence, or anything else. Companies usually take the easier route because it's easier to justify a promotion for a higher-paid position.

SEEK SUPPORTIVE EMPLOYMENT, SEEK ONLY ESSENTIAL ENGAGEMENT.

Supportive positions are those that bring money to your business. Such positions are directly linked to profits and losses. Sometimes it's challenging to distinguish essential roles from non-essential ones. In general, support positions are considered the core of business activity.

These positions include salespeople, sales managers, production managers, marketing managers, plant managers, supervisors, and general managers. Supportive roles encompass lawyers, planners, data processors, research and development specialists, as well as administrators of all kinds. Carrier services directly assist the business in acquiring and retaining customers. On the other hand, support services attract and retain customers indirectly. Services that do not attract or care for customers are unnecessary.

In most companies, the majority of people are employed in administration and sales. People working in administration are not less talented. However, they do not hold the reins of the business. The company does not rely on them.

Accept a support position only if it is clearly temporary and offers more money. Make sure which positions in the company are pivotal. Make sure you have chosen the right one.

TAKE CARE OF YOUR OWN PROGRESS.

An astonishing number of managers believe that their career is planned by the HR department. They are convinced that companies have big plans for them. Some people think there is a predetermined path up the corporate ladder, much like in the military or police. All a young manager needs to do is diligently dedicate themselves to their tasks, and then the almighty company pushes them to the next step.

However, career advancements don't work that way.

Large companies do not have plans regarding future leaders. It is doubtful whether anyone has such plans at all. Your fate and your career depend solely on you. You need to know what your goals are. You need to create a plan to achieve them. It's crucial to be aware of the skills and experience required to reach the top of the company. You are responsible for acquiring them.

ACQUIRE AND RETAIN CUSTOMERS.

Customers are the lifeblood of any business. Everyone should know this. They continue to say, "The customer is always right" and "We are at the service of the customer." But only a small part of the employees, through their actions, show that they believe in these two statements. It is commonly believed that the higher an employee is in the company and the larger the company, the less they have to deal with customers.

Managers reorganize companies, cut jobs, and justify their actions by claiming that now they are "two or three steps closer to the consumer." Nonsense! There are no boundaries between the customer and the employees of the company.

Why do so few people in the company deal with customers? Working with buyers is challenging because they conflict with sellers, negotiate, make unpleasant demands, and expect their needs to be satisfied. Working in administration is simpler, more impersonal, and safer.

It is extremely important to work with today's and future customers who are a source of ideas for new products, new approaches, and processes. They alert you in advance about the quality and timeliness of your products. They are well aware of your competitors. Knowing customers means knowing the future of the company.

When the phone rings, twelve people should hurry to answer it.
The customer is king. The future director understands perfectly well that his kingdom consists of customers.

TAKE CARE OF THE STRENGTH AND ENDURANCE OF YOUR BODY.

Your brain brings you money, but your body carries it. The better your physical condition, the higher your ability for continuous work, work that will yield results.

Good physical fitness is your advantage. Ninety percent of people climbing the corporate ladder are not in shape. With good physical condition, you can start work earlier, take fewer breaks, and finish your workday with enthusiasm.

Moreover, you will sleep better, have more energy, and tire less frequently. You will have more energy, and you won't fall into depression.

You will have the necessary energy and motivation to engage in sports in the evenings and weekends, attend movies and theaters, and participate in volunteer activities.

How you take care of improving your physical condition is up to you.

DO SOMETHING DIFFICULT AND SOLO.

Regularly engage in something Spartan and individualistic. Do what most people avoid. This will give you a sense of toughness and perseverance that will set you apart from others. This way, you will be mentally prepared for battles in business.

It's tough and lonely to study fashion design late at night, especially in winter when everyone else is asleep. Or go for long-distance runs early in the morning (or during lunch break).

Chop wood, write, sit in the garden, read "King Lear," but do it yourself. Do something solitary.

All great and successful athletes remember endless hours of rigorous training without reward. The same memories exist for directors of large companies.

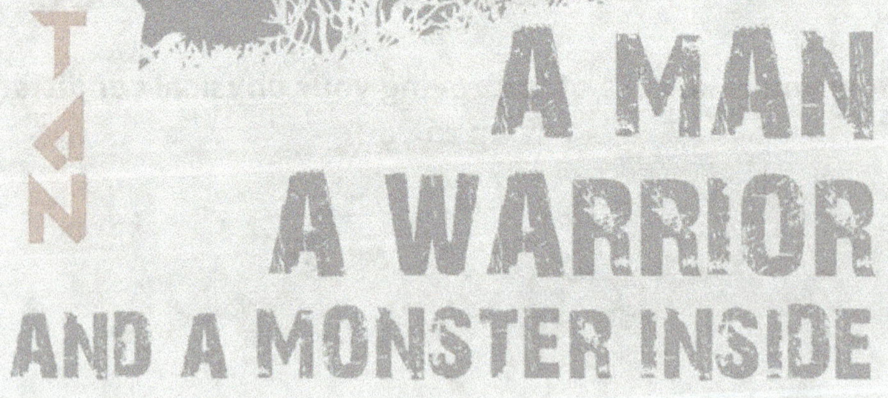

NEVER WRITE A DEROGATORY REPORT.

Never write a report that scolds, condemns, underestimates, insults, or in any way might offend a colleague. Never write a rude, condemning, or unkind report. Never send a report written in anger or offense.

The business world is very interconnected. People progress up the career ladder, change companies and jobs, have influential friends worldwide. All of this happens throughout your forty, fifty-year career. Companies merge and become independent. An enemy you create can appear anywhere and anytime.

Don't fuel the fire between yourself and competitors. Spend your energy on positive things.

ALLOCATE AN HOUR EACH DAY FOR REFLECTION.

Set aside an hour each day for planning, dreaming, drawing, contemplating, and reflecting. Think about your goals. Explore different options. Dive into problem-solving. Jot down your ideas. Mentally prepare for a phone sale or a major presentation. Learn how to do what you need to do. Develop extrasensory abilities.

Do this every day, at a designated time, at your desk.

Don't do this while running or driving, shaving, or taking a shower. Don't schedule this hour of reflection during work hours, as something will inevitably distract you.

Keep your notes in a special "idea notebook."

WRITE AND USE AN "IDEA NOTEBOOK."

Buy a notebook that you like and always keep it in one place – in a desk drawer or in your portfolio. Write down all your ideas, plans, goals, and dreams in it. You can also use the idea notebook to record tasks that you need to perform daily, weekly, monthly, and annually. Good ideas always have their time. Then start implementing them as you wrote in your idea notebook.

STAY AWAY FROM DRINKING WITH COLLEAGUES.

Don't go for drinks with colleagues after work. It's a waste of time and money. Instead, enjoy a glass with your spouse or a friend. Avoid drinking alcohol for breakfast. It's even better if you indulge in physical relaxation or focus on work during snack time.

When on a business trip, skip cocktails before dinner and go for a run or swim. Visit the sauna, take a shower, and dress up for dinner. Never get drunk with someone connected to your company in any way. It's a sign of weakness, showing that you can't control yourself.

DON'T SMOKE.

When you smoke, people around you find it unpleasant. By doing so, you risk offending non-smokers, which can harm your career. Even smokers don't like the smoke, ash, cigarette butts, dirty ashtrays, and the smell of smoking.

In addition to well-known reasons against smoking, there are specific reasons to avoid it in the business world. Smoking is a waste of time. It's a self-centered activity. However, if you want to progress, you must remember others, their needs, and desires.

Smokers may control themselves with smoking, or at least it seems so. Winners control the business.

There's nothing wrong with smoking a cigar alone or with friends. Smoking an expensive cigar in the presence of your boss is a mistake. It will create the impression that you are vain, indulging in your desires, and have or spend too much money. If your boss suggests celebrating with a cigar, decline. You probably haven't earned the right to smoke a victory cigar yet.

DON'T ATTEND WORK PARTIES.

There are no official parties. The office, workplace, or office space is not a venue for social gatherings. Never attend such work parties. It won't hurt to decline them. Don't offend people by criticizing the parties or publicly expressing your opinion. Politely excuse yourself and simply don't go to the party.

Don't participate in picnics with colleagues if you can't bring your spouse. If you attend alone, you risk appearing in a bad light due to others' actions.

If there's an unwritten rule of "come or you'll be upset," leave. Drink only non-alcoholic beverages. Don't stay for more than forty-five minutes. Thank your boss for the invitation and say goodbye. If someone asks why you're leaving, say you're busy with your wife, parents, fiancée, doctor, music teacher, or personal trainer.

Parties should be enjoyable. Enjoy them with friends. Stick to the old rule: "Never mix business and pleasure."

FRIDAY - THE DAY TO ASK, "HOW ARE YOU?"
Every Friday, go to lunch with someone whom you believe can provide you with useful information about work, and ask them, "How are you?" These are people who do not work in your department. They work in different parts of the company and contribute to the accomplishment of your work tasks. If you work in sales, it could be an assistant sales manager or someone calculating individual shares in the product's price. If you work in marketing, it could be someone working in production, public relations, or somewhere else. In any company, there will always be someone who can provide you with valuable information.

If you don't know who you need for your work, ask. Business is like a machine: every part of it needs to work. Every detail must be lubricated for the machine to work smoothly. Find out who the key person is in your work, regardless of their position. Do everything possible to let them know that you need them and appreciate them. Gain a new ally in the company every month.

CREATE ALLIES AMONG COMPETING SUBORDINATES
Your colleagues in similar positions are your competitors for career advancement. Support from competing subordinates is crucial. This support will be helpful even if your opponent intentionally or unintentionally causes you harm. If they speak well of you, their subordinates will feel good because they already trust you. If they speak disparagingly of you, they won't believe him because they already have a good opinion of you.

ADDRESS PEOPLE BY NAME.
For most people, there is no sweeter sound than the correct pronunciation of their name. Memorize the full name of the person and inquire about them. Find out what they do and why their work is important. If you take this seriously and people notice that you are genuinely interested in them, you will succeed.

It is very effective to bring visitors (clients, job applicants, friends) to tour the office or plant. Introduce them to your colleagues and, in addition to names, tell them how important their work is in the company.

Your colleagues will appreciate your attention, and they will be pleased that you put effort into making others aware of and appreciate their work.

ORGANIZE VISITS WHERE YOU INTRODUCE PEOPLE WHO PERFORM WELL.
Sometimes you invite a person holding the highest position to visit your department and take a look around. Before the tour, create 8x12 cm cards for each colleague. Write on them in one or two lines what makes each person particularly successful. The cards should serve as a guide for your visitor so that they can personally thank and praise each person.

In such a tour, everyone becomes a winner. The boss will enjoy the undeserved positive response from your people, and at the same time, he will be better informed about the work. Your people will be delighted that they are valued, and they will have more motivation. Everyone will appreciate you. Group friendliness will be your achievement.

TRY A LITTLE HARDER THAN OTHERS

Ted Williams and Joe DiMaggio, two of the greatest baseball players in history, each trained much more than all their teammates combined. Alexander Graham Bell conducted over a thousand experiments to create the prototype for the telephone. The difference between a successful person and an average person is measured in centimeters. The sales agent who makes more phone calls, the copywriter who writes more drafts, the carpenter who builds more ships, and the market researcher who conducts more interviews—these are the ones who become the best.

ARRIVE AT WORK 45 MINUTES EARLIER, LEAVE 15 MINUTES LATER

If you want to be the first in your company, start by being the first at work. People who are late to work are assumed to dislike their job, at least that's what the higher-ups believe. People don't show up twelve minutes late to a movie. Starting early also gives you a good overview of your company's employees.

Don't linger at work until ten every night. This implies that you can't keep up with others or that you have an unhappy personal life. It's better to leave the office fifteen minutes later. During this time, organize your work for the next day and tidy up your desk. Ninety-five percent of people will leave before you anyway, so your reputation as someone unafraid of work won't suffer.

Throughout your career, there will be countless circumstances preventing you from leaving work early, perhaps due to flight times, meetings, or year-end closures. Let this be another reason to dedicate more time to your family in the upcoming year.

If you come to work forty-five minutes earlier and leave fifteen minutes later, it adds up to one extra hour of work per day. That's two hundred fifty hours more work in a year or a month, allowing you to progress quickly.

DON'T BRING WORK HOME FROM THE OFFICE

The time you spend at home should be dedicated to your family, education, planning, expanding your interests, or teaching your children to play the guitar. If you consistently bring work home, it means: 1) you can't manage your time effectively, 2) you're boring, 3) you're wasting precious non-work time, or 4) all of the above.

A very busy and successful advertising executive, SHE always brought home mountains of paperwork. Her elementary school daughter, seeing her mother perpetually occupied with extra work, innocently asked her one day, "Mom, are you one of the less talented ones?"

It's typical for directors to always bring work home. However, aside from reading irrelevant reports and outdated documents (such as annual reports), they don't do anything at home. If your superiors notice that you don't bring home extra work (even if you carry a briefcase), they will likely entrust you with more projects and responsibilities. And that's a good thing.

most importantly, without fanaticism.

just don't be so fanatical.

EARN AN "INVITATION TO THE INNER CIRCLE"

At the top of every company is the "Cosa Nostra," a tight-knit, exclusive family. This is the group that truly decides who becomes a leader and how long someone stays in the company. You must be invited into such a group. You can't just climb in through your work or special achievements. You need more than just talent. You must acquire the same qualities that distinguish members of the inner circle from others.

These characteristics usually vary from company to company. In some companies, all leading sales agents might have been with the company since its inception or might be members of the founder's family.

Find out who is a member of the inner circle and why. Learn what qualities are required to become a participant. If you can't acquire these qualities, consider whether you can still accept someone who is different from you. If you can never acquire the necessary qualities, go to a company where it is possible.

If all bank executives were once in the credit department, make sure you're there too. If all members of the board are engineers, you should become one too. If the people at the top were former sales agents, focus on sales.

You can become a leader without an invitation to the inner circle, but it won't last. Within three to five years, you will lose your position either to an influential manager, a majority shareholder, or the board of directors.

AVOID INTIMACY DURING TRAVELS

Most people aspiring for career growth in companies use any opportunity to get closer to the management during business trips. They believe that the path to the top is paved by taking care of the president or CEO, ensuring their well-being, and showcasing how intelligent they are. Good managers evaluate people based on their work results, not their ability to explain. Good managers are usually very busy, and if you're not working on their projects, they will prefer to focus on something else in ten minutes rather than on you.

Use your time on business trips to work. Summer is a time for business, so travel alone. If you travel with the company director and work all summer (as it should be), he may think that you want to impress him. Or, worse, if he has even a hint of guilt for dozing off or flipping through a magazine during the flight, he might feel threatened by your diligence. If you have to fly on the same plane, please, fly in a different class.

The time you spend at the hotel is also working time. If you travel with the management, they may feel obligated to invite you to dinner. If they don't invite you, they will inevitably cause you pain. In any case, you will lose valuable working time.

DINNER IN THE HOTEL ROOM

Since you are traveling alone and will be spending days with clients or representatives from other companies, your evenings should be free. (If you are invited to a business dinner, make sure to close a deal. Set goals and strive to achieve them.) Dedicate your dinners away from home, family, and friends to work. Have dinner in your room. Do what you need to do. Compile reports, read research, check emails, and reconcile expenses.

Dining in your room will save you time and money, and enhance your independence. It extends your working day and expands your workspace. Make plans, watch a game or a movie, order a bottle of good wine, and get to work.

Also, have breakfast in your room. Order breakfast at a specific time. Get up early, exercise, get dressed, and start working. Don't waste time waiting in line for breakfast. Don't read the local newspaper. If you are on the West Coast, call the East Coast. Plan your day. Set your goals. Send an email. Fix a few things.

If you have a working breakfast (and such meetings are excellent), set the agenda and goals and strive to achieve them.

HANDLE BUSINESS IN THE PLANE, NOT POCKET BOOKS

Traveling by plane does not distract you from the environment, and there's no rush. Calls on the plane are rare, so no one will disturb you. Plan your work on the plane according to the time you have. Bring work that you can easily accomplish during the flight. Set specific goals for each flight.

EDIT YOUR "NAMES FILE"

Get a good-sized address panel or notebook. From the first day of work, record the names of people you meet, get acquainted with, and work with. Also, note where they work: in management, marketing, supply, or as freelance authors. Use a pencil, as people constantly change jobs and phone numbers. Every six months, send a message to people you see less often: former classmates, colleagues, and others. Always ask people for their business card, and they will ask for yours. Now you will be saved in their file. Save a copy of the file and use it throughout your career. You create simple connections with people. No one else will do it quite like this. Invest in people.

SEND HANDWRITTEN MESSAGES

Currently, impersonal communication prevails. We have faxes and emails, answering machines, voice recognition computers, pagers, talking cars, and digital telephone signaling systems. Someone else writes greeting cards for you. No one else writes their own Valentine's Day cards with "roses are red, violets are blue."

Handwritten messages stand out. They are a remedy for the digital world. After such messages, people will remember you as someone with good habits and taste. These personal messages never go out of style, even if they come from a noble past.

There are many occasions when handwritten messages are required: thank you notes, invitations, congratulations, condolences, short messages like "Perhaps you would be interested in...", "Excellent presentation...", "Dinner was superb...".

Visit a well-stocked stationery store and order a roll of high-quality personal cards and envelopes. Place the box on your desk, along with a few cards.

Send one handwritten message per week.

DON'T BE TOO FRIENDLY WITH YOUR BOSS

The relationship between you and your supervisor is professional, not friendly, so there is a certain boundary. Do not cross the boundary by being too familiar with your boss. Don't even allow your boss to cross it. Many people think it's wise to become a personal friend of their boss and try to achieve that. They arrange meetings, try to get invited to various parties, join the same clubs as their boss, and so on. These are not investments in a successful career; they are substitutes for talent. And it's obvious. Get to know your boss well. Familiarize yourself with their problems, plans, personality, character, strengths, and weaknesses, and everything else. Always be ready to help, both professionally and personally. But don't become too friendly. You can become friends later when you work in another company. The same goes for your subordinates.

DON'T HIDE MAJOR PROBLEMS

Major problems always come to the surface. If they were hidden, even unintentionally, they have more serious consequences. Those who concealed them always take it badly, whether they were involved or not. Those who discover them always come out better, regardless of responsibility. If you become aware of a serious problem, mistake, or inaccuracy, report it immediately to your supervisors and colleagues. The longer you wait, the more serious it becomes. A major problem can be an opportunity to showcase yourself. Break it down and explain it in detail. Assess the potential damage. Describe possible scenarios. Propose potential solutions. Ask for help. The last part is important, but it's also crucial for you to act as an independent reporter, observing the situation. Describe the problem as if you are not involved. President John F. Kennedy remained untarnished after a public television appearance where he addressed the Bay of Pigs crisis: "It's my fault, we messed up, does anyone have questions?" His influence even increased.

REMEMBER: WORDS ARE FREE, ACTIONS ARE PRECIOUS.

Raise your profile within the company. You can do this by working on high-profile projects or projects that are particularly dear to your superiors. Identify where the problems are. Work on finding solutions, and then implement them. Write your proposals and present them well.

Don't boast about how good you are. Instead, prove it through your actions, again and again. Remember: "Words are free, actions are precious."

Ted Levitt from Harvard Business School wrote, "Creativity without effort is irresponsibility." Ideas mean nothing if they are not implemented.

Only a few people actually execute ideas, so those who succeed in this area are eagerly awaited to take on something else.

Choose projects where you can showcase yourself. Presentations to management, training newcomers, and addressing sales agents are well-noticed. Identify them and work diligently on creating truly outstanding presentations.

Success is I% plan, 99% action.

ALWAYS MAKE TIME FOR VACATIONS.

A businessman who boasts about never taking a vacation is either a fool or incompetent. You need to choose or create a department, job, or area of responsibility where work can flow smoothly even without your presence, or else you won't even be able to go on a business trip.

There are several business reasons why you should take a vacation. If you go to the right places, it will be easier to meet people who will want to help you. Vacations are also an opportunity to experience different lifestyles, modern perspectives, and benchmarks, diverse ways of doing business, and literally broaden your horizons. This time could be spent writing a book, learning photography, or making Tuscan risotto. It's also a time for reflection and planning. At the same time, a planned vacation forces you to work seriously before you leave, tackling mountains of work.

Always plan your vacation in advance. Plan your winter weekends a year ahead and inform your superiors in a timely manner. Never cancel your vacation. Never leave your phone number for vacation. Be curious and travel to different places. Always go on a journey.

NEVER DECLINE A DIRECTOR'S REQUEST.

Time management books for managers may disagree with this rule, stating that never refusing a request weakens control over time. But never turn down a request from the company's director, even if he asks you to water the potted plants in the corridor.

Listen carefully to the request. Your director may offer a solution without understanding the root of the problem. But in reality, he wants a solution to the problem. Evaluate his solution to ensure it is adequate. If not, come up with your own ideas to truly solve the problem.

Regardless of what he asks you to do, offer more and faster than he expects, and show a bit of your own ingenuity. People who do their job well get the most valuable work.

NEVER SURPRISE YOUR BOSS.

Bosses don't like surprises. The work environment, their superiors, insightful competitors, and other subordinates already provide enough unknowns, so they don't want any surprises from you, neither good nor bad. Above all, they want you to promptly share your experience. They want to be accountable to their superiors about the status of projects, the resolution of the latest crisis, and the developments. Your boss wants it to seem like he has everything under control, that he has an understanding of what is happening. Leaving him in the dark is disrespectful to him and the entire company.

If you surprise your boss, he will stop trusting you. But you definitely need to earn his trust. Whether he is good or bad, he has the greatest influence on your early career.

Your boss is usually better informed about company events that don't concern you. Even a surprise made with the best intentions can be destructive if it involves events that you misjudged due to ignorance.

Put yourself in your boss's shoes. No surprises.

MAKE YOUR BOSS SUCCESSFUL, AND HIS SUPERIOR EVEN MORE SUCCESSFUL.

For real progress, a significant step up the ladder is usually necessary. You will have the greatest opportunity for career advancement if you take care of your boss's work. He cannot move forward if there is no one to take his place. If your boss looks successful, he is more likely to get a promotion, but if he looks successful because of you, he will still want you to be his assistant. So now you have the opportunity for career advancement.

Your boss cannot arrange your promotion without the approval of his superiors. If you make his boss even more successful, your chances of promotion will increase. The manager of your manager is always a key figure: he usually takes more interest in your career and can influence it more than your immediate supervisor. This is especially relevant if your boss remains in the same job.

Your leadership will appear more successful if you anticipate their needs and problems and make extra efforts to find solutions. Make sure they are always in the loop. Always finish the work before the stated deadlines. Always do a little more. Look at the work through their eyes. Help them by taking care of their projects.

NEVER ALLOW YOUR LEADER TO MAKE A MISTAKE.

The best thing that can happen to you and help you rise is to work for someone who will be beneficial to you. Such a boss will prepare you for his position, so after his promotion, you will also have the opportunity to get promoted.

Never allow your boss to make a mistake that could jeopardize his chances of career advancement because it directly endangers yours. Do not allow him to make a mistake that will harm the company because it can hinder the prosperity of the company... and the better the company does, the more resources are available for rewarding work.

If your boss needs more information to better perform his job, ask for it. In the absence of the boss due to illness, provide him with a brief report. If the manager's presentation lacks evidence, supplement and support it.

Do not link the mistakes he makes to him personally. Do not say, "You made a mistake" or "There is a mistake in your report." It is better to address mistakes like this: "Maria, there may be an error in this calculation. It seems that the costs are understated. If we write ten dollars instead of eight dollars per hour, the calculation will be more realistic."

Appendix: Tell everyone who works for you—outside or inside the corporate paradise—that they should never allow you to make mistakes. Make sure your boss knows about this rule of yours.

VISIT THE LIBRARY ONCE A MONTH.

Leave the office and spend one working day every three to four weeks in a public or university library.

Carefully study your schedule there and organize urgent projects. Think through every detail. Complete administrative work. Break down large projects into smaller, manageable parts. Update personal matters with new information. Edit your idea notebook. Write all welcome messages, client letters, and thank-you letters.

A day of uninterrupted work in the library will allow you to accomplish ten times more than you would in the same time at the office. The thought that you have done so much work will inspire you. You will feel that you have work under control, which will motivate you to work regularly in the office.

DO SOMETHING IMPORTANT EVERY YEAR.

A company leader should be knowledgeable, educated, and interested in many things. You should also see solutions to your problems in the light of other cultures, knowledge of nature, and art. You need to know how to concentrate your energy and train self-discipline.

If you learn a new important perspective or approach every year of your life, you will be prepared to run a business. Learn a foreign language, Chinese cuisine, or photography. Write a book, grow orchids, raise canaries. Learn to play a well-known and popular song on the piano.

Make a list of what you would like to do in the next ten years. Do not limit yourself. When you say you are too old to learn tennis, you are actually saying you are too old to grow, expand your interests, or run a business. If you have little time, you cannot count on being able to handle work that requires twice as much responsibility.

Prove your ability to grow and develop.

DRESS FOR DANCE.

A very wise school director once disagreed with the president of the student council, who wanted to change the strict dress code for school dances. "When we dress for football, we play football. When we dress for dances, we dance." The same applies to business. When we are dressed in business attire, we mean business.

In different places, companies, and factories, different dress codes reflect different cultures. This is correct because every culture should be respected. For example, in Puerto Rico and Hawaii, business is often conducted in long-sleeved shirts. Field directors sometimes wear hats and work boots. Factory managers wear protective goggles and lab coats. These are exceptions that are easy to understand.

Practice the position of a director, which also includes how you dress. There is no need to spend a lot of money on custom-made suits and be obsessed with fashion. Buy a book on business attire and familiarize yourself with it.

NVEST IN PEOPLE.

Hire the best people. Attract, encourage, train, and reward the best.

Companies that think they will save money by hiring people they can afford are doomed to fail... if they haven't failed already. It's better to hire an extremely capable person for sixty thousand dollars a year than two mediocre ones for twenty-five thousand dollars each. Also, don't skimp on emotional returns. Reward winners with trust, independence, praise, freedom, and encouragement.

Company leaders understand that people are the driving force behind the company. They never forget this fundamental truth. A general is nothing without an army. If people in your company support you, trust you, believe in you, and respect you, they will lead you to the top. But it's true that people only give what they receive. They are like mirrors. If you trust them, they will trust you in return. If you respect them, they will respect you. Many leaders fail because employees perceive them as insincere, dishonest, cowardly, or unreliable. People tolerate the mental, physical, cultural, and even moral flaws of their leaders. But they never tolerate xenophobic behavior.

When hiring people, consider the following: first, honesty, which should be the top priority. Second, the "I can do it" attitude is crucial. Third, for smart people. If individuals are aware of the limitations of their knowledge and the fact that they have to put in ten percent more effort than master's or doctoral candidates, this is a true indicator of intelligence.

When you find such a rare person, invest in them. They will know it and repay you handsomely.

People are not foolish. They are in the business world not to create financial losses and enemies or make mistakes. All they need is reasonable investments in them, in these people.

I OVERPAY PEOPLE

If an employee needs to be paid five dollars per hour, he knows about it. If you pay less, you will spend much more money to prevent the consequences. The employee will feel deceived, so he will not put in a drop more effort than necessary and will not want to work overtime. At the same time, he will try to find a way - psychological, physical, or economic - to punish you for unfair pay.

If an employee needs to be paid five dollars per hour, and everyone knows it, pay him fifteen percent more. It will pay off twice, as the employee will do everything possible to justify your trust.

Short-sighted managers do not understand this. They believe that low salaries reduce expenses and that people should be happy to have a job. They believe that people are not worth as much as their salary. It is true that at all levels of the company, there are people who are not worth their salary. Get rid of them because they are taking money from people who are really doing good work. The salary of those who contribute nothing to the company can be distributed among the rest.

You cannot save money by paying people poorly. People pay you back and make a profit if you invest in them. If a bank investment brought you a twenty percent profit, would you cut expenses (reduce investments)? On the contrary, they would invest even more capital.

Your business will be much better if you hire a few good, well-paid people than if you pay the same or less to a larger number of people.

STOP, LOOK, AND LISTEN.

Directors think. They don't do anything hastily or without careful consideration. They think about what can play a role, observe, test, and listen. They pause and look. They stop before saying the wrong word. They stop before making a rash decision. They stop before sending an offensive letter. Then they look and listen a little more.

If you want to become a director, you need to practice the skill of stopping, observing, and listening. It's very challenging to listen, especially to aggressive, energetic, lively people. Train yourself to always be in a state of high acceptance. You also need to hear the unspoken, just like Sherlock Holmes heard the dog that didn't bark. Learn to listen to the language of eyes, hands, and gestures. It's essential to pay attention to clients, suppliers, bosses, colleagues, company sales agents, competitors—in short, everyone.

Listening can be learned and practiced. If someone is talking, stop what you're doing, look at them, and listen to what they're saying. Good listeners are considered people with whom you can have a conversation. They equate the ability to listen with wisdom and intelligence.

Listen, listen, and listen again!

BE FULLY COMMITTED TO YOUR COMPANY.

If you want to become a director, you must fully dedicate yourself to the company, its products, or services. You need to understand and believe in the company's mission. Embrace the company culture and then contribute to it convincingly, publicly, and without hesitation.

Whenever possible, use your company's products and consistently recommend them to others. Do not work for a company if you cannot openly talk about the advantages of its products. If you don't believe in cigarettes, firearms, champagne, or yogurt, don't work for companies that produce them.

Buy shares in your company if they are available. Purchase your company's products only if it makes sense, and recommend them to your relatives and friends.

Cynical attitudes towards the company are characteristic of ordinary people, not future directors.

———————❖———————

FIND AND FILL THE GAPS IN KNOWLEDGE.

In business, if someone says "I think," "I'm sure that..." or "This is my opinion," it usually means they don't really know anything. Identify what you don't know or what your company doesn't know—these are "knowledge gaps."

Don't be deceived by the eloquence of insightful colleagues who just talk and never leave the office. Find the facts. Consult with customers and users.

Certainly, professionals in a specific field don't know everything, but they are always willing to work diligently to acquire the specific data they need.

WORK, WORK, AND WORK AGAIN.

Most people in the business world never work hard. They constantly create the appearance of work, rushing and pretending to be busy. They diligently read reports, attend meetings, write extensive protocols, fill out forms, and waste time. It's the "seesaw syndrome" effect—lots of movement without real accomplishment.

Good workers spend the same amount of time but use it intensively. They do the heavy lifting. They engage with the project. They gather data. They think about how to achieve the goal. They work out all the details of the process. They work and think about all the crucial issues. But most importantly, they think. And they truly do it.

A "seesaw" type of person prepares for a history exam by reading eight chapters ten times in seven hours. On the other hand, a working type breaks down the chapters, distills the essence of the information, and memorizes all eight chapters in seven hours. Success in projects doesn't expire. But it's all due to the work.

TREAT EVERYONE WITH RESPECT.

People are more than just a crowd; they are individuals. Among them are mothers, fathers, coaches, charity workers, volunteers, religious teachers, and those who care about the well-being of society. They are capable of a lot if you value them, and even more if you encourage and appreciate them.

Good managers make people feel that they are:

Asked, not coerced.
Paid fairly, not underpaid.
Valued, not controlled.
Individuals, not just staff.
Enthusiastic about their work, not coerced into it.
People working with tools, not just tools.
Workers, not just a product.
Gaining, not just costing.

Approaching everyone with respect and recognizing their individual worth fosters a positive and productive environment. Acknowledging people's contributions, encouraging their efforts, and expressing gratitude can go a long way in building a healthy and motivated team.

HEVER LOSE YOUR NERVES OR PATIENCE.

"Nothing gives a person a greater advantage over another than maintaining composure and sound judgment in crucial moments."

Outbursts of anger, helplessness, impulsive decisions, finger-pointing, and cowardice are signs of panic. Good directors do not lose their temper and avoid flashes of anger. They know how to control themselves, thus maintaining control over the situation.

Pressing is a key stage in winemaking. During this stage, for several weeks, grapes are selected for harvesting, their quality is checked, accepted or rejected, and juice is extracted, which will later become wine. An error at this stage can jeopardize the entire annual wine harvest, leading to a damaged reputation for the producer, a decline in prices, and profits.

A few years ago, in the midst of pressing at a well-known winery, a manager called another manager and informed him that the grape grower had resigned. The director immediately understood the potential damage but remained calm, took a few moments to think, and then asked, "What would you do if the grape grower had died and not resigned?" The manager explained the procedure for selecting a new grape grower. "Then do that," said the director, and the new producer continued the tradition for the next fifteen years.

If a colleague directs an inappropriate remark towards you, do not allow yourself to be provoked, but there is nothing wrong with laughter. Those who are on your side will be offended no less than you. Those who do not react will sense that you are in control of the situation. Others will see you as the winner in the position. Don't get angry. Even when anger is justified, those who get angry evoke disgust from those around them.

Learn to keep your blood cool. Remind yourself that you need to keep calm. If you have ten seconds to make a decision, spend nine on reflection.

EXPRESS YOURSELF IN SIMPLE LANGUAGE.

It's important to learn how to communicate. Your message should be clearly expressed. Poor communication is the most common cause of wasting time and money. Millions of dollars spent on advertising yield no results. Millions of work hours are wasted on unnecessary or incorrect tasks. Millions of written reports go unread.

Business communications must be precise, thorough, and entirely understandable. Both written and oral expressions, especially work instructions, should be clear. Wordy, boring communication filled with exaggerations and jargon is a waste of time.

If people don't understand you, they will do it wrong. Dedicate as much time as needed for complete mutual understanding. The irony of communication is that companies often talk about the lack of communication. Good communication requires a lot of effort because it demands significant receptivity from the listener or reader. It requires adapting to the needs of the audience, their mental representations, available time, data reception, and educational level. To communicate clearly, follow these rules:

Make sure the letter or message is truly necessary. Clearly define the message's topic.
Choose the simplest means of expression. Learn about things and gather all the information. Create a mental model covering all points of the message.
Carefully edit your message.
Shorten and modify it to one page. Use language that readers will understand.
And here's one more good basic advice: think for three hours and write for one.

GIVE PEOPLE WHAT THEY DESERVE.

Trust everyone 100% with their work. If you have five people working, and each of them gets 100% for their work, you will get 500%. These are facts.

It's like building a house: someone is fully responsible for the foundation, someone for the roof, someone for electricity, and the builder will be fully responsible for the sum of these parts for the entire house.

Many managers don't understand this. They think they will suffer if they trust their employees too much. They believe that some credit is due to them, especially for a beautiful roof. That's why they appropriate it. They tell their boss, colleagues, and even the person who did the work that only they truly bear responsibility.

Those who take credit for others' work are insecure, dishonest, and known for it. Even the cleverest ones are always exposed. At first, it's ignored by the people working with them, and then it slowly spreads throughout the company.

Give credit where it's due, and you'll become known as someone worth working for. Your people will work diligently because they'll be working with the idea that you acknowledge their merits.

REWARD EMPLOYEES UNEXPECTEDLY.

If someone excels, especially if it goes beyond their duties, reward them. (Don't wait for the company to approve it.) Don't publish the criteria for receiving the reward. Don't let people know that a reward system exists. Don't follow the rules. Distribute different amounts at different times of the year.

Anyone working for you knows that a reward can come unexpectedly. And everyone will work harder to increase their chances of being rewarded.

BE POLITE TO EVERYONE.

Always be polite to everyone. Be kind. Never abuse your position. Don't show disrespect to your superiors. Don't smoke in a colleague's car. Don't smoke during meetings or meals. Don't swear or use profanity. Don't put your feet on office furniture. Don't place your briefcase on the negotiation table. Treat your office, your colleagues' offices, cars, and all company property as if they were your own.

Always be punctual for meetings. Don't leave representatives or visitors waiting in the hallway. Don't make people wait by the phone. Don't waste other people's time. Be especially careful with your subordinates' time. Respect is a great business trait.

Always introduce yourself, your spouse, or anyone else clearly and distinctly. Always introduce your subordinates to the company's management.

Say "please" and "thank you" every time.

DEMONSTRATE EMPATHY AND APPRECIATION.

People who have a positive view of themselves and their work will strive to perform at their best. If they work for you, with you, or alongside you, they become a driving force for good work. Compliments or expressions of attachment to people will make them feel good. But you must be absolutely honest about it. Practice and remember the following statements:

Please.
Thank you (a good manager should say this at least twenty times a day).
Remember the NAMES of employees.
You did an excellent job.
I appreciate your efforts.
I hear only the best about you.
I'm glad you're collaborating with us.
I need your help.
You deserve this recognition.
Congratulations!

GLORY AND SPLENDOR.

Diplomas, prizes, trophies, awards for the best sales agent, membership in the board of directors, and the like symbolize fame and splendor. Offices with good locations and high earnings are also part of the splendor. This is the visible part of success in business. But there is also the invisible, behind-the-scenes part: the daily pressure that many people do not notice, appreciate, or make.

Daily pressure is what matters and brings fame. It's the hours of homework, early mornings, weekend trips, checks and double-checks, trials and errors, and endless hours of progress, inch by inch, hidden in splendor.

If you ignore the daily challenges, you won't gain either glory or splendor.

CORRECT, REORGANIZE, TEST.

Business mistakes cost so much money that almost every successful company with more than a thousand employees avoids innovations. About 97 percent of people in companies fear change and innovation. However, only new ideas and new products create new customers and serve as a source of viability and survival for a company.

Creating new products is a labor-intensive process, regardless of a company's rhetoric; it's almost always mutually challenging. Being innovative is unique, but what management primarily needs is quality.

Not much works perfectly from the start. Successful plays on Broadway were not staged after the first project. Developing new products is a maze of errors and dead ends. Ideas require refinement, mechanical processing, polishing, and trimming to become viable.

Support a good idea. Spend some resources. At the initial stage, make sure you spend as little money as possible. Do everything possible to provide feedback. Process the concept. Edit it to better suit your target audience. But most importantly, try. Try this and that. Do not distribute, organize meetings, or write reports, but dedicate yourself to a new idea. Create something based on the concept, create a prototype, distribute samples. Then process the idea again, rearrange it a bit, and try again. If the idea is bad, you will find out. Discard it. But if it's good, now you can propose it to the company. Now you can handle the risk and compete successfully for investments.

SLOWLY OR QUICKLY BUT CONFIDENTLY, IT GOES FAR.

In the business world, there is a myth that it is worth being an aggressive, confident, spontaneous manager who makes one lightning-fast decision after another. This style is acceptable if the decision can be changed or canceled without significant damage or if time is very limited due to the threat of a catastrophe, such as a fire in a factory. Decisions made in haste are risky.

Decisions come in two types: reversible and irreversible. Those who can distinguish between them are halfway to becoming good managers. Decisions that can be canceled can also be changed. They can be made relatively quickly because they have less impact, and if they are wrong, they can be corrected. The company must live with irreversible decisions.

Learn what it takes to make reversible and irreversible decisions. Typical examples of reversible decisions include:

Job duties,

Advertising graphics,

Pricing,

Non-decision,

Committee powers,

Company rules,

Choice of insurance company,

Selection of a telephone service provider.
In general, irreversible decisions include:

New company name,

Acquisitions,

Selection of top managers,

Building construction,

Selection of computer systems.
Always think quickly and learn things quickly to be able to make decisions quickly.

INVEST IN GOOD THINGS.

If you have found a good thing, no matter how mundane, old, or proven it may be, invest all your energy in it. Success comes not only from solving big problems, developing new products, or implementing radical changes. The financial commitment of a company is to ensure maximum returns for its shareholders. You do this by determining which customer needs are profitable and which can be satisfied. If your customers like something, don't change it. Do not change the headline, ingredients, name, price, advertising, or anything else.

Disney understands this. Mickey Mouse was first introduced to people fifty years ago. Understanding the charisma of Mickey Mouse, Disney invested significant resources to make him an American icon. Today, Mickey Mouse greets visitors to the Disney park, appears in movies and books, sells everything from dolls to glasses, and remains a star in Disney stores.

Procter & Gamble never tires of advertising that Ivory soap is "99.44% pure." In fact, this slogan has been used for over a hundred years, and Ivory soap remains one of the best-selling soaps in America. Strength lies in consistency. Do not change the formula for success. Better invest all your energy in it.

THE IDEA MATTERS, NOT ITS ORIGIN.

Always be on the lookout for good ideas. Be completely impartial about their origin. Ideas can come from customers, children, competitors, other companies, or taxi drivers. The origin of the idea does not matter. What matters is who will execute it. Many managers do not understand this.

Creative people are productive. They immediately recognize a good idea. With their personality, they contribute to its development and completion. Creative people do not ask, "Whose brilliant idea is this?" They do not underestimate ideas and those who propose them. They do not allow themselves to be distracted.

Truly creative people understand that they have only one brain, no matter how creative they are. Therefore, they listen to others to get as many good ideas as possible. If they listen to a hundred people, they will multiply their creative abilities a hundredfold.

— ❖ —

AVOID OFFICE GOSSIP.

Some managers believe that the road to success is paved with dead colleagues. They go to great lengths to embarrass or belittle their colleagues. The cruel ones use barbs, and the more sophisticated ones use daggers. They are often sly. They are always on your heels or at your throat. Their actions are evident. They only survive in weak companies.

There are rumors that the management in the company is bad. The reward system is usually unfair and unclear. There may even be problems at the top. Instead of fighting or competing for new clients, employees fight among themselves, trying to be the boss's favorite and wasting time.

Don't waste your time. Use it to create and achieve goals. Let your actions be your policy. In good companies, this matters.

Learn about intrigues last. Don't let them drag you in between. Don't let people whisper something "confidential" to you. Don't ask, don't answer, don't engage with them. Don't speak ill of anyone. Don't perform. Instead, say, "I don't know."

Dedicate yourself to your work.

BE ORGANIZED.

A little vanity won't hurt. Take care of yourself and maintain an attractive appearance. Stay in good physical shape. Have a neat hairstyle. Avoid worn-out, faded, or cheap clothing. Take care of your overall appearance and eliminate any signs of negligence.

Stay healthy. Think rationally. Take vitamins. Exercise and eat properly. Recognize unhealthy stress, learn to reduce it, and relax. Have a general health check-up every year.

Make an effort to have a radiant smile. Brush your teeth and ensure fresh breath. Fix your teeth and get bridges if needed. Ensure you have beautiful hair, hands, and nails. Get rid of dandruff and avoid strong scents.

Regularly clean your shoes. If you like, insert a fresh flower in your lapel. Make your stride lively.

Be in a good mood. And keep smiling.

LEARN FROM YOUR ROLE MODELS.

Most people can count their best teachers from kindergarten to the present on one hand. The same goes for coaches and mentors, especially in the business world. Great leaders are rare. There are many good people, but truly great leaders are a rarity.

Great leaders teach without preaching and praise the right things. They embrace challenges and set honest goals. They are individuals who let people grow without subjecting them to the hindrances of harsh judgments, public criticism, or corporate bureaucracy. Some of them might be independent and have their quirks or even be a bit eccentric. But all of them have vast experience, work hard, and think deeply.

Look for such people early in your career. Work for them. Observe them closely. Judge how they handle criticism and problems. Learn how they do their work.

STAY WITHIN THE BUDGET.

Complete every job on time and within budget. Advancement in your career is ensured by doing what is expected of you. Going over budget causes problems. Companies always strive to cut costs, so exceeding the budget exacerbates the situation.

Don't look at political institutions or government road construction departments. Even at the lowest level in a company, it's essential to stay within the budget. The manager's task is to know their projects well and figure out how they will implement them within financial constraints.

Limited budgets require creativity, skills, and ingenuity. Working with such a budget is a challenging task. Find new and more affordable ways to execute your plan. You will improve the company, and your efforts will be appreciated.

NEVER UNDERESTIMATE YOUR OPPONENT.

Your opponents can be your competitors, competing managers, or anyone in the company. They may appear to be: a man, a woman, overweight, an athlete, old, young, a beauty, or a charismatic person. Opponents can be talkative, gossipy, impostors, or honest people. Don't be deceived by their appearance or reputation. Don't be overconfident or vain. Don't be fooled into thinking you can predict everything.

Never underestimate the intelligence, perseverance, and skills of your opponent. Never underestimate their capacity for good and evil, including duplicity, dishonesty, or cunning.
If you underestimate your opponent, you may find the chair slipping away from you. But if you overestimate them, you might pleasantly surprise yourself.

TAKE DOWN THE INSTIGATOR WITH ONE SENTENCE.

One of the biggest threats to your career is the instigator who manipulates company politics for their own success and glory. You can find them anywhere. It could be your boss. He is always dishonest, greedy, and cunning. His target is new colleagues entering the company and those on the rise. He will try to undermine any potential rivals. Managers climbing up the ladder are his most common victims since they take more risks, making more mistakes.

The instigator instinctively understands Mark Twain's insightful observation about manipulating truth. In his essay "Advice to Youth," Mark Twain wrote: "The truth is, that when God builds a fool, the devil provides a brain. But a good fool doesn't live long in this world of lies."

If you pay attention, you can quickly identify the instigator. No one escapes his intrigues. This also makes him vulnerable.

When a conversation with a colleague leads to the instigator, which is bound to happen if you are the target, simply say, "Certainly, Mr. X spares no one."

Your colleague, who knows Mr. X, will assume he recently became the target himself. Thus, the instigator will be disarmed.

BE AMONG THOSE WHO ASK, "WHY NOT?"

People who mostly ask themselves, "Why should I?" always end up with: "I should do this," "I could do this," or "I would do this." Such people are usually very idle and never take risks. Because they fear losing, they never plan to win. They are dull individuals. They never burn out and always come away without a scratch. They never suffer a last-minute failure. They are never pioneers in their field and never become initiators of a new movement. Among such people, you will never find someone truly significant.

The question you should ask yourself is, "Why not?" Join the winners. Every time you say to yourself, "I shouldn't have done that," you should know that you will have ten times more opportunities when the results show that you should have done it.

Without courage, there is no glory.

THE PLAN SHOULD NOT BE PERFECT; IMPLEMENTATION SHOULD.

If you wait for the perfect moment, the perfect new product, or just the right circumstances, you will never start. Even the best products of the best companies needed improvement. If the idea is better than any other and if it maximally meets market requirements, then implement it. If there's a better way, don't wait for it to become better. Don't let the "perfect" become the enemy of the "better."

Dedicate yourself to the development and presentation of ideas, paying attention to every detail. Leave nothing unfinished. Bring your product to the market without delay. Make sure the price, advertising, etc., are adequate. Regardless of what new thing you want to achieve success with—whether it's a product, a manufacturing process, or real estate—it's the perfection of execution that determines success or failure.

RECORD YOUR FAILURES WITH ATTENTION AND PRIDE.

Mistakes are milestones. They indicate work in new and unknown areas. They are learning materials. Write them down in your "idea notebook." Determine what exactly you did wrong, where you slipped, what made you do it. What made you say something wrong? Were you angry, behaving immaturely, bragging? Did you carelessly complete an assignment, overlook a detail that seemed unimportant, or just procrastinate? Make yourself work and implement the plan.

Recall the history of your mistakes. You probably won't repeat the same mistake. Write down what you learned and how you will address similar problems in the future.

Admitting your own mistakes is a sign of self-confidence and self-awareness. It indicates a willingness to try new approaches and take risks. Those who work also make mistakes.

Records of mistakes usually represent memories of very successful people.

LIVE TODAY, PLAN FOR TOMORROW, FORGET YESTERDAY.

Yesterday cannot be brought back, so don't even try. Don't worry about yesterday and don't rejoice prematurely. Deal with today, which matters. Today is the day you want it to be. Plan for tomorrow. It will be a good day.

ENJOY AND HAVE FUN.

Business itself is serious enough. If your job doesn't bring you joy, you need to change it or find a way to derive pleasure from life.

If you can make work more interesting for your subordinates, they will work with greater enthusiasm, more creativity, and will be more satisfied with their work and life in general. A work environment that seems to be in decline, full of pressure and seriousness, is stressful and ineffective.

A leader who can maintain a sense of humor and morally entertain colleagues will always be surrounded by a motivated and happy workgroup. A sense of humor is a sign of intelligence, and this quality is highly desirable in leaders.

———————✤———————

TREAT YOUR FAMILY AS THE MOST IMPORTANT CLIENT.

It's easy to let your business career take up all your time and energy. The more you dedicate yourself to work, the more work you'll have. However, neglecting your spouse or children would be a mistake.

You need family support because they will help you in your career. You need an enthusiastic spouse who understands that you may have to give up some things. Let your family become your ally in achieving your planned future.

Include your family in your daily plan. Attend as many sports matches with your children as possible. Plan vacations. If you're taking your kids to a party, leave work a bit earlier. Keep family matters on your to-do list. Time spent with family will pay off tenfold.

When your wife or children talk to you, put down the newspaper, turn off the TV, look up, and listen. This way, you'll deepen family relationships and, at the same time, practice active listening. Moreover, it's polite.

Be as responsive to your family as you are to work or a very important client."

WITHOUT GOALS, THERE IS NO GLORY.

In hockey and football, there are no victories without goals. A goal is a goal and is the result of successful, well-directed efforts. Without goals, there is neither victory nor glory. The same applies to business and life in general.

You need to set goals. Time-management books assert that goal setting is the first step to gaining control over your time. Goals shape plans, direct energy, and allocate resources.

Write down your goals in an 'ideas notebook.' You should define at least two goals: one for business and one for life. Break them down into goals you want to achieve in twenty-five, ten, five years, and one year. Divide annual goals into monthly steps, and then into smaller weekly steps.

Create a list of urgent tasks for days, weeks, months, and years. They should include all the tasks necessary to achieve your goals. Also, note in your daily plan tasks that will bring you closer to your long-term goals. This will guide you in the right direction.

If you don't set goals for yourself, you won't achieve them. Goals beget goals."

"DO NOT FORGET THE WIVES OF SUBORDINATES.

A successful career requires a whole person. Your success depends primarily on the people who work for you. If you lighten the burden on people, they can carry it longer. Spouses can make the work of subordinates easier or more difficult. They can understand and support their husbands, but they can also annoy and complain. If your subordinates have to travel or work overtime, their spouses can either support or completely hinder their work. Spouses can be crucial allies in the company or dangerous enemies.

Common sense usually hints at this, but spouses are often forgotten and excluded.

Do not forget the families of your subordinates. Whenever you have the opportunity, personally thank them for their support. When you send people to an international exhibition, send flowers to their spouses. If you are traveling and a colleague feels obliged to invite you to dinner, invite his wife as well.

Occasionally reward a subordinate with a "weekend for two" for excellent work.

Do not forget their spouses. It will make everyone a little happier."

"LOOK AT YOUR WORK THROUGH THE EYES OF A SALES AGENT.

One of the oldest truths in business states: 'Nothing will happen until someone sells something.' Accountants won't calculate, manufacturers won't produce, and managers won't sell... until the item begins to sell. There are a few products that sell themselves. Most products require sales. Someone needs to get the order, place the product on the shelves, and convince the customer to spend money on the product. Sales are crucial for the company.

Regardless of your role in the company, regardless of the company you work for, and regardless of the product or service the company provides, you need to look at your work through the eyes of a sales agent. They face customers directly and have immediate contact with them. They listen to their complaints and have to handle rejections.

Make a decision to sell. Sell whenever there is an opportunity. Be sales agents for travel services. Call customers. Attend supplier meetings. Monitor their training. Find out what's going on. You will gain merits in the sales field, which is a strong link in any company. At the same time, you will earn the approval of sales managers, who are a powerful group in every company. You will learn what motivates sales agents and what discourages them. You will get to know customers, and this knowledge is a source of greatness.

Work for the sellers, and they will work for you."

"BECOME AN INDOMITABLE SALESPERSON.

You must learn to sell in a way that no one can talk you out of it. If you want your department to work on Saturdays, get your manager to approve your latest plan, or work on an important project, you need to get an order. There are thousands of books on sales. Let's delve into some of them. Your task is to become an indomitable salesperson, capable of winning every order.

You don't need to be an artist or a eloquent speaker to learn to sell and take orders. But you must do the following:

Identify your client's needs,
Identify the product features that will satisfy those needs,
Develop a firm, steady, and persistent approach,
Make a 'sales call,'
Do everything possible to get the order,
Be ready to make as many calls as necessary to get the order.

Persistent and patient individuals understand that the numbers are in their favor. They know that one-fourth of contracts are closed with a simple request for an order. The remaining three-quarters of orders will only be taken after the fourth or one of the subsequent calls. Ninety percent of sales agents don't even ask for an order. Ninety-five percent of all customer interviews have nothing to do with sales; it's just communication and entertaining customers. Therefore, indomitable salespeople understand that persistent and patient individuals have few competitors in this field. They understand that success depends on making more calls and asking for orders.

Persistence, patience, and the right approach are qualities of an indomitable salesperson."

"DO NOT BUILD AN EMPIRE.

Many managers mistakenly believe that they will reach the top if they have as much money and people working for them as possible. In reality, companies need managers who can get the job done with minimal costs and a small group of people.

Never complain that you are expected to do more than the budget allows. Don't become a manager who constantly has to hire people and expand their department. Don't let a lack of resources and materials be an excuse for poor performance or failure.

Forget about building an empire. Progress and power are achieved not by those who possess people, but by those who truly create."

"FOCUS ON WORK, NOT ON PAPERWORK.

Modern companies face a serious dilemma. They demand high performance, hampered by lengthy procedures and paperwork. They need innovation and intelligent risk-taking. They need entrepreneurship. They must direct all their resources—money, time, people, and production—toward the market. However, companies are drowning in paperwork and office work.

Large companies fear internal entrepreneurial spirit. They find it difficult to deal with personalities creating businesses. Most managers cannot handle a freer style, free from rules and lengthy procedures, characteristic of people full of ideas—people creating businesses. Large companies require monthly reports, detailed cost calculations, form filling, call recording, quarterly reports, year-end reports, hundred-page annual business plans, contingency plans. They have a mountain of other demands that consume time, money, and energy, but don't ring the cash register.

Don't let yourself be buried in a pile of paperwork. Don't agree to the demands of a company that ties your hands. Monthly reports are unnecessary because they are verbose, boring, and reminiscent of 'creative' writing from the distant past. Don't write them. If they insist, let everyone who works for you take turns writing it. Everyone. Each one should write what they think is smart. Don't encourage the reproduction and reading of such reports. Don't even think about reading it yourself.

Also, don't write reports about meetings that everyone just attended, don't write reports about business trips (detailed expense reports and business rights), and anything that does not directly improve your business."

"TEACHING IS ABOUT LEARNING AND LEADERSHIP. Leading people.
Always seize the opportunity to teach within the company. Regardless of your job, you can always enhance the company by telling others about your work (and the work of your department), why you do your job, how you do it, and everything else you are responsible for. If you work in payroll or HR, teach new sales agents about it. If you're in charge of advertising or market research, tell producers about the impact of advertising messages on their work and how to create surveys for clients.

Prepare well for teaching. Preparation requires homework, organization, execution, and practice. Through the learning and discipline required for such preparation, you will deepen and supplement your knowledge.

———————✤———————

Good preparation and practice are the keys to a successful presentation. Good work will earn you a professional reputation at work and throughout the company. At the same time, you will learn more about people and areas in which your company operates. Thus, you will have a strong impact on a wide range of people.

Teaching will help you understand why your responsibility is so important to the company. Your audience will begin to understand that you are indispensable to the company."

"DO NOT FEAR IDEA DESTROYERS.
Companies are filled with idea destroyers who come from various positions, have different characters, perspectives, and sizes. Idea destroyers say things like, 'We've already tried that,' 'Management won't like it,' 'We can't afford it,' and many other statements that nip any risk in the bud. One of the most common phrases that encourages inaction is 'It won't fly.' It is especially disheartening when you hear this from senior and experienced people in the company who are supposed to know something. Young people who aren't afraid that something is impossible become disappointed and wary when they hear such comments. Practitioners who work to make their grim predictions come true thus maintain their 'status quo.'

During the oil embargo of the 1970s, when car manufacturers were forced to increase fuel efficiency, one of the major car manufacturers proposed significantly reducing the weight of the car to senior and more experienced engineers. They couldn't meet the demand because they were trapped in old ways of production. They said it was impossible, too expensive, and would greatly reduce the safety of the car. So, the company hired many young, inexperienced engineers who removed excess weight from cars simply because they worked without constraints.

Don't give up. Don't give up on the idea. People with ideas create businesses. Creators rise to the top. Don't let idea destroyers bring you down to mediocrity. Think boldly. Implement ideas with enthusiasm and determination. Fight opposing opinions. Even a small success will attract investors and like-minded people from all departments of the company.

Think of idea destroyers as something useful, as encouragement. Let their doubts be an opportunity for you to learn more about the issue. Make extra efforts to overcome the obstacles in the way of implementing your idea."

WHAT ARE THE MAIN TASKS?

Invest money in yourself, in your education and development. Do not skimp on knowledge, understanding that by generously managing money, according to the law of reflection, you will receive generosity from the world.

Learn to sell yourself, your knowledge, your ideas. Develop skills in effective self-presentation.

Develop the art of speech, the power of words. Improve the ability to express thoughts and influence others.

Build an environment that brings you closer to your best version. "Tell me who your friend is, and I will tell you who you are..."

Develop a creative mind and imagination.

Take care of your brothers and sisters.

Understand the cycles of your destiny, the ups and downs. Avoid lingering in crisis states, depressions, or victim mentalities.

Learn to meditate, listen to silence.

EFFECTIVE LEADERSHIP

PRACTICE THESE 6 DISCIPLINES

EFFECTIVE LEADERS DO THE RIGHT THINGS

- Effective leaders set priorities well and focus to do first things first
- They avoid crisis by planning for the future
- They do not hesitate in saying no to requests that do not line up with the company's goals and vision
- They strive to do the right thing through self awareness and acceptance of their blind spots

EFFECTIVE LEADERS VALUE CONTRIBUTION

- Effective leaders execute from a place of trust, understanding, learning, contribution, courage and not from fear, ego, control, perfectionist
- They value integrity and respect people who have the desire to do the right thing
- They do not involve in wordsmithery or other pretentious mechanisms to achieve what they want
- They believe in contribution and inspire others by themselves being a part of it

EFFECTIVE LEADERS SYNERGIZE

- Effective leaders open lines of communication, bring the collaboration and synergies required across multiple functions to devise an effective, forward looking plan
- They focus on goals and output
- They are transparent in their decision making process

EFFECTIVE LEADERS LEARN TO MANAGE THEIR TIME

- Effective leaders identify where their time goes and take control of it by cutting back on areas which place unnecessary demands on their time
- They organise and devote this time to future looking activities
- They make the best use of their time by attending to conflict at its source and not delaying in the hope that it will resolve itself

EFFECTIVE LEADERS HIRE AND GROW PEOPLE

- A strategy without the right people to execute it is of no use. Effective leaders understand this very well and spend a

EFFECTIVE LEADERS MAKE

Magic Word

sorry

please

welcome

thank you

excuse me

YOUR TEAM is a gift. Like a gift, you may not have asked for it. Even so, always show your appreciation for it.

Look. Listen. Experiment. Share your ideas, skills, and passion. Take risks, work, and be a friend.

Gifts are fun, so don't forget to play! But if you *break it*, do your best to *fix it*.

Sometimes the best gifts are those you didn't want. It may take time to see your gift's value. **Wait and keep an open mind, give it a chance.**

The surprise is half the fun. Enjoy what you discover **TOGETHER.**

Positive workplace culture, joy, family, goal-setting, time management, leadership, gratitude, influence, effective communication, sales skills, continuous learning, avoiding bureaucracy, innovation, dealing with naysayers, personal and professional growth, self-investment, understanding life cycles.

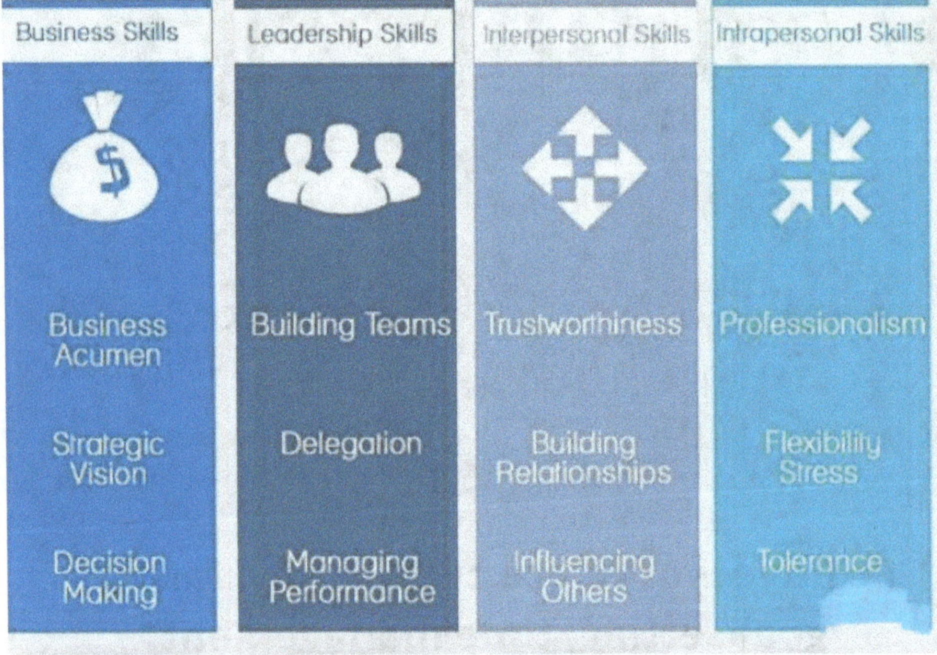

Leadership, self-improvement, goal-setting, effective communication, sales skills, positive workplace culture, family support, dealing with challenges, avoiding bureaucracy, innovation, continuous learning, self-investment, understanding life cycles, taking responsibility.

always help your colleagues

LEADERSHIP

Leadership is the ability to inspire, influence, and guide others towards achieving a common goal or vision. A leader is someone who possesses qualities such as vision, integrity, empathy, effective communication, and the ability to make sound decisions. Leadership involves motivating and empowering team members, fostering collaboration, and providing direction to navigate challenges. It's not only about managing tasks but also about inspiring and developing individuals to reach their full potential. Leadership can take various forms, including situational, transformational, or servant leadership, and it plays a crucial role in the success and growth of organizations and teams.

DON'T THINK OF COST. THINK OF VALUE.

Leadership is a multifaceted concept that encompasses the capacity to lead, guide, and influence individuals or groups towards common objectives. Effective leaders often exhibit strong communication skills, strategic thinking, and the ability to make decisions that align with the organization's vision. Leadership is not solely about authority but also about inspiring trust and fostering a positive work environment. Different leadership styles exist, including autocratic, democratic, and laissez-faire, each suited to various situations and organizational cultures. Successful leaders embrace adaptability, continuous learning, and the development of their team members. Leadership is a dynamic process that involves setting a clear direction, motivating others, and creating a shared sense of purpose to achieve collective success.

*Be the kind of
LEADER that creates
other leaders.*

EPILOGUE.

Let this be your reference book. Thank you for reading this book. Now, open it to a random page (or two). Point your finger at this chapter and start bringing it to life.

This will bring you closer to becoming a leader. For success in life, every person must fulfill the tasks of their soul.

Leadership is not about you; it's about investing in the growth of others.